To Pastor Johnson!

Best,

Juliette Oluoku-Eboh

D1282549

I

# 10 THINGS
# I KNOW

# 10THINGS IKNOW

## Juliette Okotie-Eboh, PhD

**Dere Publishing, Inc.**
Detroit, Michigan

*Cover by Terrance Palmer, for DP Marketing Strategies*
*Back cover photo by Michael Sarnacki, for New City Photographic*

This book contains stories in which the author has changed some details in order to protect the privacy of others.

Published in association with the marketing agency of DP Marketing Strategies, Inc.
P.O. Box 3773 Southfield, MI 48037
www.dpmarketingstrategies.com

**10 THINGS I KNOW**
Copyright © 2016 by Juliette Okotie-Eboh, PhD
Published by Dere Publishing
Detroit, Michigan 48215
www.thedrjuliette.com
10thingsiknow.com

Library of Congress Cataloging in Publication Data
  Okotie-Eboh, Juliette 2016
  10 things I know/ Juliette Okotie-Eboh, PhD
ISBN 978-0-692-34052-3
1. Self Help––Popular Psychology. Self Care.  2. Success––Psychological Aspects.

Printed in the United States of America
10 9 8 7 6 5 4 3 2 1

# 10 THINGS I KNOW
By Dr. Juliette Okotie-Eboh

## Table of Contents

# Author's note

The primary objective of this book is to strengthen your self management and self awareness in a way that will allow you to enhance your personal and professional life. Moreover, I want you to consider yourself a leader and give you tactics for holding yourself, as well as others, accountable as you work toward your vision of success.

This book is not designed just for men or just for women. It's written for the highly-educated and the GED graduate. This book is for everyone.

Allow it to be a fun dialogue between you and I! Enjoy the conversation, reflect on your own thoughts and see how you can make these Ten Things work for you!

*Juliette Ohotti-Eboh*

# Acknowledgments

I would like to acknowledge and thank my parents, Lawrence and Aldena Thorpe.

I would like to acknowledge and thank my sister Margaret Williamson, my daughter Margaret Okotie-Eboh and my two nieces Juliette Murdock and Aldena Williamson.

Blessings and gratitude to the Juliettes, the Margarets, and grandmother Maggie who are pillars in our family, and continue to live on in our hearts.

Thank you to all who assisted me in this project, especially Diane Palmer.

Love never ends. . .

# *Chapter 1*

# Get a Life
# & Own It

# assess your life and get one that has purpose

Have you ever heard someone say flippantly, "He needs to get a life?" Most times the statement is made when it seems as though the person is simply drifting along or doing something that is in opposition to others. Often, it's easier to shine a light on someone else rather than stand in the spotlight ourselves. What if there's more meaning to the statement than people ordinarily give it?

I challenge you as you start to read this book to access your life and get one if you don't have one already! Here's what I mean by that. Life is not just a sequence of things that you do every day; there's more significance to the journey than that. You need a vision for your life. You need goals to reach and steps outlined to get you there. You need people in your world to hold you accountable to those goals. The vision must be crafted, with a plan to accomplish it. The vision for your life should be positive and motivational. It should answer the internal question, "What inspires me?"

## DESTINATION: HAPPY PLACE

The vision that you have for your life should be

inspirational, yet abstract. If your goal is to find your happy place, then the vision for your life serves as a road map. It becomes your guide to get there. You have to think about it in broad terms and then narrow it down. It may require that you expand your circle of friends or your network.

## Who's in your social network?

I strongly recommend creating a social network that works for you. Consider all areas of your life (family, friends, hobbies, interests, social organizations, work, etc). This will help you to evaluate where you are now and how the people and activities you fill your life with, fit into your personal vision for the present and the future.

Assess the strength of these relationships and whether or not they can help you to reach your goals. In essence, you are crafting your Empowerment Zone, the path to owning your life.

*One of the mistakes many of us make is looking at another person's life and saying, "I want a vision like that."*

One stop along the way could be getting a better job or finding a relationship that adds to you and doesn't take away from you. Your plan would now include: goals, ideas, opportunities and people that will help you to arrive at the destination called happy for you.

The key to crafting a successful vision is flexibility. If the vision that you have for your life is to be happy, then you would be motivated by that desire. Keep in mind that a flexible vision gives room for change because things don't always pan out as we hope. For example, you may land a job and your hope is that the job will give you exactly what you need to move forward, but it simply may not work out. The elasticity that you've built into the vision gives more credence to the fact that happiness may take the form of something else.

Over the years the vision may change. It's a very normal process. A vision is like a vessel. You can put things into it and take things out of it. You can amend it when necessary; after all it's YOUR vision. It's your life. As you grow and discover more about yourself, your vision can change. As life presents you with a set of colorful circumstances, your vision may change. Still, your vision should keep you motivated. If you're motivated then you're more apt to own your life rather than giving someone else the deed to your world.

## Custom Made vs. Off The Rack

One of the mistakes many of us make is looking at another person's life and saying "I want a vision like that." It's ok to admire another person's life plan, but you've been given a life of your own. It's unique. When considering another person's life, some things may be similar but nothing will be the same. Your vision should be custom made with all the bells and whistles that are authentic to you. You can't create your vision based on what others want for your life either. I have to live my life and you have to live yours. We can't live for each other. It's ok for you to be honest with yourself and start designing the "one of a kind" life you desire.

A huge detail in creating your custom vision is embracing the fact that it will take time to arrive at the destination. The awareness that things will not happen overnight, helps you to escape the overwhelming sense of disappointment that can come as a result of what appears to be delay. If possible, try to avoid the temptation to put a timestamp on every goal. If the decisions that you're making are aligned to the vision you will arrive at destination "happy" on schedule. Trust the process and keep moving.

Your vision starts within you and works its way out of you. It becomes the reality for your life. You'll have to see it in your mind before things can ever materialize. You can't live it, have it or be it until you first see it from within. So, what do you see for your life? Are you willing to take ownership of your life? From the broken homeless man walking the streets asking for a quarter to the broken business executive wearing Prada, both at some point had a vision for life. Perhaps their brokenness came as a result of being derailed and separated from their own visions.

# CONSIDER THIS!

Remember, you own it. It's a lifelong commitment. Make a decision today to OWN your life.

What will you do?

_____

_____

_____

_____

_____

_____

_____

_____

How will you live? _____

_____

_____

_____

_____

_____

_____

Your vision will require your patience. Write your vision statement. _____

_____

_____

_____

_____

_____

_____

Here's a list of things you can do to Get a Life and Own It:

- See it happening.

- Keep it alive.

- Make steps every day toward your destination.

- Be patient with yourself and the process to becoming.

- Enjoy the journey.

- Get a life and own it!!

*Chapter 2*

# Report to
# Your Position

# report to
# your position

There are times when you can't figure out who's on first. You look at your marriage after several years and you're feeling flat and bored. Your spouse is in between jobs and fighting depression. Is this the time to give in to the extra attention you've been getting at the gym from the opposite sex? No, it's time to report to your position.

You're at work asking the question -- Why are we re-organizing again? This is my third boss in two years? What am I to do?  My best advice is to pull out the organizational chart and report to your position.

Reporting to your position is vital for personal and professional success. It's that inward conviction to be who you signed up to be. It's the determination to stay true to your purpose and calling. It's the foundation you stand on when the winds of change and adversity blow as they do in all our lives. You don't waiver or fall, you REPORT TO YOUR POSITION.

## DECLARE INDEPENDENCE!

If  the office politics are murky and you don't know what "side" to choose, then report to your position. This tactic is your personal declaration of independence that keeps you on track until the dust settles.  No matter if you are at the bottom, middle, or top of the organizational chart, or even if you are the president or CEO, this is an effective tactic and can help you side-step tough situations. Declare your independence. I'm free and things aren't happening to me. I'm happening to them. Define the things that will guide how you perform. Reevaluate the goals of the corporation. Shine through the chaos by reporting to your position and performing well.

*Reporting to your position is vital for personal and professional success. It's that inward conviction to be who you signed up to be.*

Here's a sample declaration of independence that you can adopt into your daily challenge.

> I am a good human being.
> I will perform well for my company.
> I will never stop striving to be a better person.
> I will always seek out new opportunities and I am committed to helping others.

Allow these affirmative statements to guide you through the debris and help you to maintain your focus.

When we focus our attention on the things transpiring within the office rather than what we are responsible for, problems can occur. Think about it this way. If you don't report to your position, perhaps they will find someone who will.

# THE TAKEOVER

Years ago, after being on my job for six months, the company experienced a takeover. The tension in our office at that time was at the top of the Richter scale. People were naturally concerned about whether or not they would still have a job when they arrived each morning. There were major concerns about how we would "fit" into the company's new business model. In the halls of the office, there were whispers, blank stares and an involuntary awareness that everything around us was changing. The sound of offices being packed up in boxes, as professionals were being relieved of their duties was unusually loud.

On this particular day, the interim CEO of the company strolled through the office. He stopped and asked one of my colleagues, who was the Chief of Staff to the president that had just been fired, "So what do you do?" Her response embodied her willingness to report to her position. She responded by saying, "Anything you want me to do right now." Needless to say, she kept her job, and was promoted the next year to a Vice President position. Today she's sitting in the former President's chair, running the entire organization.

## Your Position Under Pressure

How you respond under pressure is critical. You must have a plan before your crisis. You will have to commit to standing tall in the area where you've been given responsibility and think on your feet. During this company takeover, I was affected as were so many of my colleagues. My vision for where I was going within the company was decimated.

Under the new company structure I was told that all decisions in my department were to come through one of the consultants leading the "turnaround" team. I decided that my department still required my leadership. So, I led. I announced to my team that we would host a weekly breakfast with the new decision maker. Each week we gathered for breakfast around the table and pitched our ideas for different projects to him. We invited his feedback. Over time, rather than going through the red tape to make decisions, the authority to lead my department as I saw fit was tossed back to me.

During that time, I had no control over the company takeover or the external elements that came with it, but I did have control over my actions. I chose to be responsible and report to my position, and several months later I was promoted. I declared my independence. I had aligned myself to the opportunity that was flowing down the pipeline to me. It's not enough to show up but, you must perform.

# THE SMARTEST YOUNG WOMAN I KNOW

My only child and daughter Margaret is my sunshine. She brightens my days and has brought me a joy and fulfillment like I never imagined. It's because of her that I choose to report to my position every day. I often ask people I mentor and coach, "What makes your feet hit the floor every morning?" For me as a single parent, the answer is Margaret.

When she was five years old we were blessed to purchase our "dream" home on the eastside of Detroit. It was no mansion, but for the two of us, a new house with a large backyard was a dream come true. To afford the home, we found the best public school in the area for Margaret to enroll in. Soon we discovered she had  learning challenges.

How was I going to afford her the best education

possible? There was no question that I wanted a quality education for her. I wanted her to have the best resources to ensure her success. I had to position myself in a way that gave her a wide platform to stand on. She gave me the power to perform.

She is by far one of the smartest young women I know. Her courage is contagious. It helped me to eliminate any excuses about what I thought I couldn't do as a parent. She needed me and I needed her and all of the other trivial things in life had to take a back seat so that we could find joy and ensure that everyday was a success for her.

## THE CALL OF DUTY

In the United States Army, failure to report to duty on time, leaving your duty post, or being absent from the place that you've been assigned are major offenses. The ability to show up and be present and on time is one of the most fundamental requirements of a soldier. The army has to be able to trust that the soldier has respect for authority and will not put the safety of his/her unit at risk. The soldier's inability to comply with the standards and regulations of the army put him/her in a position to be punished as a court-martial directs. In life and beyond, it's important that you report to your position. Yes, you must show up and be ready to perform!

# Consider This!

Ask yourself…

Am I present mentally? _____
_____
_____
_____
_____

Is my attention divided?_____
_____
_____
_____
_____

Don't make the mistake of giving your attention to something that doesn't deserve it. If you make this mistake, it's possible that someone else may be standing in your position when you decide to return.

# *Chapter 3*

# Reward Yourself

# reward
# yourself

Have you ever battled with thoughts of feeling unworthy, insecure and uncertain about your life? Life by nature presents challenges and circumstances that leave us feeling inadequate. It's part of everyone's story.

Through the years I've overcome feelings of self-doubt by telling myself and treating myself like I'm worthy. When you really believe that you're worth it, you treat yourself better. You deserve to take care of yourself. You deserve to have fun in your life. You deserve to feed your body the good stuff. You deserve to be invited to the meeting to present your big idea. You deserve to have a voice in the world. Being good to yourself must become your new normal.

## CHALLENGE YOUR PERSPECTIVE

If you've ever fallen prey to a series of setbacks and disappointments in your life, you know that it can leave you feeling low and if you're not careful, the negativity attaches itself to every word you speak and subsequent action. You have to tell yourself: "No more negativity. I will respond positively to myself and challenge my perspective about what's happening to me and around me." By pushing past the negativity that has grown into a nasty fungus over your thoughts, you will see that there is great

*Being good to yourself must become your new normal.*

value beneath the surface of your smile and you deserve all of the good your life can handle. Put on your rose-colored glasses and view yourself and your life positively. Sometimes our life just needs a makeover.

# BODY MAKEOVER

Life keeps moving even when we take breaks. As the years keep coming, we do not get younger. As you age it's important that you are good to your body. You can start with changing your

---

*Always dress for where you're going, not where you are.*

---

unhealthy eating habits and adapting a workout regimen into your daily schedule. Although, I typically work 14 hour days, I manage to squeeze in a workout regimen. It's important for me to keep my body in shape. It's one of the gifts I give to myself even when I don't feel like it. I believe that I'm worth it so I work at it. Now, let's keep it real here, guilty pleasures aren't always bad, as long as they aren't everyday right? You don't need a lot of money to make small changes. Early on, I couldn't afford a gym membership, so I purchased a Yoga videotape. When my daughter was young, skating was my exercise of choice. I'd take a few laps around my subdivision at night, and before I knew it the children in the neighborhood were on wheels behind me. I had to start somewhere, and you should too. Eliminate the excuses. Just do it. Start now.

## SHOPPING THERAPY

 A new pair of shoes always makes my world better. I love shopping. I love being a woman and enjoying nice things. You don't have to shop designer brands to fill your closet, but you can still reward yourself. Even on a budget you can give life to your wardrobe and reward yourself.

Here's a harsh reality. People see us, before they hear us. Your wardrobe at times will serve as your cover letter and could prevent you from opportunities because you simply don't look the part. Don't be cheap with yourself. Cheap thoughts give you cheap results. Make an investment in you.

I have the honor of mentoring a few professional women. I remember chatting with one in particular who felt stuck in her career. Nothing seemed to be moving for her. I listened carefully as she shared her thoughts on where she was and what her career goals were. After she had the opportunity to download all that she was feeling in her heart, I shared this simple truth with her: "If you want to be a Director, you have to look like a Director." I encouraged her to give her wardrobe a facelift. I suggested that she purchase a few nice pieces, and use black and white colors for the foundation of her wardrobe. She purchased a pair of quality shoes and a nice handbag. Shortly after that she passed by my office dressed in black and white, with a nice pair of shoes and matching handbag. I smiled. Two months later she was promoted to the position of director. The position was available, the job announcement was obviously made—but she had already begun the application process by looking the part months ahead. It's really something when you think about it. Always dress for where you're going, not where you are.

## TRADING SPACES

I believe that our living and workspaces are reflections of who we are. It's been said that the state of your space, reflects the state of your mind or well-being. Is this true for everyone? I'm not sure, but here's another thing I know for sure. It's your space and it does say "something" about you and it gives others something to say about you. I can recall when I worked at a university where I was given an office space about the size of a closet.

Well, they gave me a closet to work in, but I could see what it could be if I made a proper investment in that space.

I transformed the space into a place of inspiration, creativity and productivity. It was my space so I decided to reward myself by designing an office that was worthy of me sitting in it for eight hours or more each day. I was on a tight budget so I took a trip to K-Mart to start my inspirational design for my office. I purchased some paint, a new rug, a new lamp and a picture. I spent the weekend transforming the space. On Monday, when my co-workers arrived, they were in shock. The transformation of my workspace and the reward that I had given to myself got their attention. I felt like I deserved a great space to work in, so I gave it to myself!

# CONSIDER THIS!

Whether you're working to improve your health, bringing order to your finances, or preparing for a big interview—always remember that you're worth it. List three upcoming events or goals that you should re-consider your approach to ensure you reward yourself and shine. _____

_____

_____

_____

_____

_____

_____

_____

_____

_____

You deserve the best. The best moment is now and you have to be ready for it. First impressions are everything. Always present the best version of yourself the first time.

List two moments in the past when you should have presented yourself better. What stopped you from bringing your "A" game?_____

_____

_____

_____

_____

_____

_____

_____

_____

How can you plan ahead better to never repeat this action?_____

_____

_____

_____

_____

_____

_____

# *Chapter 4*

# Be Your Own
# Cheerleader

# be your
# own cheerleader

From little league to the NFL, there are a group of pretty girls standing on the sidelines rooting for their team. With pom poms, mini-skirts and the team's name branded across their chest, the cheering squad and even the fans in the stands believe that a win is possible for their team; and in some unique way their encouragement could help seal the deal. In our lives, it's important that we celebrate our victories, great or small even if we don't hear the applause of the fans in the stands.

*There has to be a pair of pom poms and a holler inside each of us to cheer for ourselves.*

## ARE YOUR POM POMS READY?

Sometimes at your lowest moments, the fans in the stands have gone for popcorn. What will you do then? Well, it's really simple. You learn to cheer for the home team. There has to be a pair of pom poms and a holler inside each of us to cheer for ourselves. You have to see the win. You must place great value on your contributions to life and celebrate your own victories. Everyday may not be a super bowl party, but every day can be a celebration of your decision to show up and give it everything you have. Celebrate the fact that you are still in the game, when others chose to retire early because of "personal" injuries.

Through the years I've created affirming statements that have become the soundtrack for my day. I post positive quotes in my bathroom, frame them on my wall and use them as screen-savers. It's on auto repeat in my mind. Do this for yourself. These statements  will serve as the motivation you need when you feel like your team is falling behind or you've experienced a fumble on the playing field of your life. These words will help to deafen the sound of negative noise and empower your belief that winning is possible today and every day.

## FAIR WEATHER FANS

Each day the win may take on a different look, but keep cheering for the home team. There are some teams in the NFL that have fair weather fans, who only cheer and show up for games when their team is winning; but there are also another group of fans called the "diehard" fans. These fans will cheer until their voices are tired. They wear the team's paraphernalia even if their team is on a losing streak. Their heart bleeds their team's colors. Here's where I'm going with this football jargon. You have to be a diehard fan when it comes to your life and the journey to your success. You have to keep rooting for the home team.

Some days you'll experience a landslide win. You'll know that you accomplished what you planned for that day. All of the meetings were favorable. You even managed to close some pending deals. This particular day it would be easy to cheer yourself on…because the win was just as you imagined. It gets a bit more challenging when nothing seems to be going as planned. Perhaps your presentation didn't go over as you envisioned in your mind or when you were given the floor to share your big

# OPPORTUNITY ±

# HOPE ±

# EXPECTATION =

# ENCOURAGEMENT

*We all have to pull on this formula from time to time.*

idea it seemed as if your brain started to move at the speed of a turtle. On the days that the win looks different than what you'd hope for, you still have to cheer yourself on. You can't be a fair weather fan for your team. If everyone leaves the game, you're still there and that counts for something really great!

So, what is it about encouragement that pushes us forward? I think it's the hope and belief that today is not the worst day of all, and the next decision has the possibility to produce a series of even greater things that keeps me going. I believe that encouragement is a gift we give to ourselves when we accept that we deserve the chance and opportunity we've been given to be our best selves. It causes us to hope and expect the best from ourselves and others. So, embrace the fact that sometimes you'll have to encourage yourself and hope for your future. You will have to know within yourself that better is possible and that you have what it takes to experience it all. Your life is your stage and you owe it a stellar performance.

# OVATIONS AND CURTAIN CALLS

After one performance of Othello, the audience gave Placido Domingo 101 curtain calls and an 80-minute standing ovation. That's the world record for the longest standing ovation ever. Wow! That had to be some kind of performance. What was it that moved the audience to respond with such passion and excitement? Was it his masculine tenor voice? Was it the conviction that pierced through every note? Was it a flawless performance? Obviously there were many hours and weeks of private rehearsals and run throughs. Were the before moments perfect every time? I'm not sure, but the performance warranted the longest standing ovation in history and 101 curtain calls.

# WHAT KIND OF PERFORMANCE DOES YOUR LIFE GIVE?

On the stage of your life, keep in mind that people are looking at you, they're listening to you and they're looking to you for direction. I tell myself all the time if you are on stage and you're going to be your own cheerleader then you've got to act the part, look the part and do it in a way that's consistent and affirming of who you are. So, I make sure that my attire matches the leading role I'm in. I make a conscious decision to monitor my actions and my words. Giving a heartless performance is never my goal. You must do the same. All of your life has been preparing you for standing ovations and multiple curtain calls. Every experience, if we allow it, serves as preparation and grooming for the spotlight.

Your early job experiences taught you how to enter the stage. The challenging times taught you when to exit and change your attire for the next scene of your life. All of your life is equipping you for center stage moments. You must dress the part, act the part, and deliver daily.

One of my center stage moments happened while I was working for the City of Detroit. I was given the task of leading a two-year project. This assignment was very important for the city and I was trusted by the mayor at that time to meet certain goals. My team and I had to ensure that the 1990 Census count for Detroit exceeded one million persons. If the numbers had fallen under one million, key pieces of enabling legislation would have been voided, such as the utility users tax or income tax collection for residents and non-residents. Detroit stood to lose up to $290 million in revenue per year if we had not reached our goal. Former Mayor Coleman A. Young trusted me to lead this project and it was a huge success. I had to lead from the front of the line. It's still one of my most proudest moments in my professional career. The spotlight was on me and I stood with confidence and worked hard to deliver the truth of where the city's population numbers stood.

## Consider This!

Don't be afraid of the lights. Stand up for you.

List two to three instances in the past when you could have been more vocal in taking credit for a job well done?

_____

_____

_____

_____

_____

_____

_____

_____

_____

Why did you shrink back? What caused you not to speak up?

_____

_____

_____

_____

_____

Take a bow and give yourself a thunderous applause. The curtain calls are still coming...you decided to show up and give your best....keep the cheers coming!

# *Chapter 5*

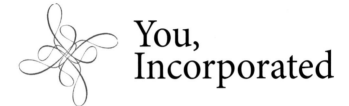

# You, Incorporated

# you,
# incorporated

The year was 1977, Marvin Gaye's "What's Going On?" was quickly becoming an anthem and I was starting a career in planning. I was young, full of vitality and ready to give the world my best. I was given a work project to prove myself. The project came with a partner. We had roughly three months to deliver. If I performed well, this could lead to a possible promotion in the department.

After the initial meeting, I worked on the project in my spare time. After several failed attempts to connect with my partner to share the workload, I decided to continue working on the project independently to insure that it was completed. The "big" reveal came when it was time to make the presentation to a few stakeholders. Everyone expressed their satisfaction with the project roll-out. Shortly after, the position announcement was made and the job was given to my non-contributing partner. I was devastated.

## JULIETTE, INCORPORATED

From this experience a new perspective emerged. My success mantra became: I'm Juliette, Incorporated. I just happened to be working for this outside company (employer) but I am the "boss of me." I determined right then that it is ultimately my responsibility to build an excellent brand and market myself. The investments that I make to develop my career, character, skill set and knowledge-base to increase my personal net worth will create value and yield great returns.

While my success enlists the help of others, it first begins with me. Envision yourself as a corporation. Let's look at the term corporation – simply defined.

> Corporation [kawr-p*uh*-**rey**-sh*uh* n]
> a legal entity created through the laws of its state of incorporation. The law treats a corporation as a legal "person" that has standing to sue and be sued, distinct from its stockholders. The legal independence of a corporation prevents shareholders from being personally liable for corporate debts.

There are a few words that stand out here: legal, entity, and independence. You, Inc. suggests that you are an established entity. You have authority and rights. You are a force within the world.

Every corporation has a high-ranking official also known as the CEO. The Chief Executive Officer is primarily responsible for managing the day-to-day operations of the corporation,

> *Your Board of Directors must be comprised of the people who motivate you to succeed.*

which includes but is not limited to hiring and firing employees, answering to a Board of Directors and ensuring the corporation remains profitable.

# WHO MAKES YOUR FEET HIT THE FLOOR EVERY MORNING?

One of the goals of the Board of Directors is to help improve the performance of the corporation. Once I embraced the mantra of Juliette, Inc. I positioned my daughter Margaret as the sole member of my board of directors. Nevertheless, my point is that your board of directors must be comprised of

*As the CEO of You, Inc. you understand that you are not defined by a job, promotion or salary.*

the people who motivate you to succeed. These people are your lifeline and the catalyst for your feet hitting the floor every morning to work versus staying in bed.

You are your own corporation. You are the CEO of your life. You are responsible for being the "creator" behind your company's vision and overall success. Keeping a child or children in mind could help you make the necessary decisions. This could be the fuel you need to make right choices. Make sense? This is so much more exciting than getting a good job or being a good employee right? We will talk more about this later.

As the CEO of You, Inc. you understand that you are not defined by a job, promotion or salary. Your vision exists outside of one job opportunity. You're not chasing a few dollars; you are competing with yourself to be the best you possible.

This is why it's important that you clearly develop the vision for your company. What does success look like for you? How will you know when you have achieved what you set out to do without a well-thought out vision? You should consistently ask yourself questions like: "Does this opportunity or feedback put me a step closer to the desired outcome?" "Will this help me to be better? Is this aligned to my overall vision?"

Consider this. The decision making process for a  corporation is decisive and strategic, not emotional and erratic. For example, If you determine that it's time to transition from the company you're working for, it would be detrimental to you to inhibit the process based on emotional statements like: "My favorite restaurant is around the corner from the office." "This job is 15 minutes from my house." "All of my friends work here." "I really like my boss." All of these things are not deal breakers. You can make more friends and entertain old ones on your personal time. You will find another restaurant that you like, and you can visit your favorite one on the weekends. You can't afford to make long-term decisions based on short-term inconveniences.

For example, if you see an opportunity that will give you a $5,000 increase in pay but the position will not help to foster the growth you desire or help to nurture and develop the skills required to accomplish your corporate vision, then the $5,000 is not an asset, it's a liability. On the other hand, there may be a position that does not yield immediate financial gain, but it is in line with the goals that you have for your corporation. This opportunity positions you to acquire the skills and mentoring you need for the overall vision of your company. Choosing the latter is strategic and decisive. It could be one of the greatest moves you make for your corporation. You're the CEO. Would you take the risk?

Every job posting is not yours to apply for. Every performance review may not be favorable. Sometimes you will rub shoulders with the politics of the marketplace. Objectivity is key. Objectivity promotes forward thinking which allows you to grow beyond the blows that come with the journey to success. The objectivity searches for a wider space to live in. It thrives outside of the box.

## MUSICAL CHAIRS

Years ago while working in an executive position, I can remember a time where thinking objectively helped me to maneuver through a transition graciously. During my tenure with this company I had five different offices. The musical office game within the corporate setting often denotes that management does not want you to be comfortable. Well, I had to make some adjustments within myself so that Juliette, Inc. could perform at its best. They moved me from office to office and each time I created a space for Juliette, Inc. to soar.

I consolidated my power with every move. I remember telling one of the managers, "Listen, it doesn't matter where I am. I can do my job from the kitchen table." My stance in that moment empowered me and removed the perceived power from the person who was facilitating the musical office game. It was a great day for Juliette, Inc.

Adopting the thought model of You, Inc. can create a healthier approach to building working relationships, dealing with difficult people or conflict, and inviting feedback. It cuts the ties to limitations that are a result of utilizing an emotional filter. Remember, you're not competing for a job. You're not in competition with the people around you. You are in competition with yourself. You are about the business of being you.

## WISE COUNSEL

As the CEO of your life/corporation; it is your job to assess the day-to-day operations of your company. You'll have to consistently make changes to promote your growth and development. In this role it's easy to become blind-sided by some of the needs because you're engrossed in the day-to-day. It's a huge responsibility, and it will require that you allow others to assist when necessary. While Margaret solely sits on my board with full voting power, I have leaned on others for counsel and mentoring when needed.

Recruit a mentor to offer insight, encouragement or counsel. These mentors or counselors can serve as a support system and resource for your corporation. They offer feedback and insight that could be very valuable.

When choosing a mentor or counselor consider people who:

1) think objectively
2) are upbeat and supportive of you as an individual
3) are trustworthy

## DECISION TO RELOCATE

Quite a few people who I loved and respected did not understand my decision. During that time I had to look at all of the stakeholders and their vested interests in my decision to determine why their response was opposite my decision. I also weighed heavily the response of two major mentors: my mother and father. They were both in agreement with the decision which neutralized the responses of the others. As the CEO of your corporation you must be able to make decisions with wise counsel. You have to consider their feedback objectively and make changes when needed.

# Consider This!

Now that you've accepted that you are largely responsible for your success and you have acknowledged that you are CEO of your life, it's time to settle into your role and move forward with your eyes wide open.

# *Chapter 6*

# Assumptions Get You Off Course

# assumptions get you off course

The resurgence of food trucks has become a phenomenon in major cities across the country. In years past, food trucks catered to construction sites and served blue collar professionals during their lunch breaks. Today, food trucks are owned and run by chefs and can be found in urban and rural areas. Interesting how times have changed, yet some things remain the same.

# MY FIRST JOB

I learned my lesson about making assumptions or prematurely judging people (and situations) when I was ten years of age. My father sold fruits and vegetables in the summer months in addition to his job in the factory at Ford Motor Company. I was his helper as we traveled during the week through predetermined residential areas in Detroit. My father, with a ninth grade education, was a very successful business man. Our food truck was a haven for fresh fruits and harvested vegetables.

At ten years old this was my first job and it's the place where I learned not to assume anything. The principles for excellent customer service and the art of treating people with dignity and respect are things that I learned while working on my daddy's food truck. These fundamentals served as the basis of my foundation and helped to steer me in the right direction when developing corporate working relationships.

---

*The principles for excellent customer service and the art of treating people with dignity and respect are things that I learned while riding on the back of my daddy's fruit and vegetable truck.*

---

On my father's food truck route we ventured through the really nice African American communities of Detroit.

I can remember the women approaching the food truck in their nice frocks to purchase their produce. My father was extremely polite and managed to connect with his customers in a very gracious way. On Saturday evening, my father and I would sort through the remaining produce and cover it in ice --- a painstaking process where of course, I complained the whole time.

*Stereotypes about people and situations will only render to you the shorter end of the stick.*

On Sunday morning our route led us into one of the rougher areas of the city where apartment buildings covered the skyline and cigarette butts lined the streets. I was shocked by the difference between the neighborhood and the people I saw in comparison to our usual customers--- it was the exact opposite of what I was used to.

Noticing my discomfort, my father gave me specific instructions once we arrived at our weekend route. He said, "The only difference about where we are today is that you won't take their groceries in for them. They will carry their groceries themselves. I don't want you going into those apartment buildings. For him that was the only difference. While their socioeconomic status may have been gravely different, they were still paying customers who deserved our respect, great service and a quality product.

Money was the great equalizer. He made it clear that we charged much less for the same produce on Sunday even though we could charge the same or even more in this neighborhood. "Today, everything we make is profit. They don't know that the peaches are a bit riper than yesterday, but I do." After he shattered my assumptions and taught me one of the greatest life lessons I'd ever learn, he turned around and welcomed the staggering customer by saying "Yes ma'am, how can I help you?" We made a lot of money on Sundays--- in fact it was our most profitable day.

# Unpack those bags

Stereotypes about people and situations will only render to you the shorter end of the stick. Our character is not only developed by the way that we think about ourselves, but how we respond to others. Not only did I learn about customer service while working on the food truck but I started to establish **business ethics and core values** at an early age. The Sunday runs on the food truck were all profit earnings for my father. We cleaned the truck as we did during the week, but we marked all of our produce at 50% of the original cost to sell on Sunday.

My father knew that the produce was a few days old, as this was the balance from the week so it had shifted from being "great" to "good" and he refused to cheat or take advantage of anyone. He was considered to be a neighborhood grocery store—with wheels. His character helped to shape mine. I am so thankful for the lessons I learned while riding and working with my father on the food truck.

**Your core values are critical to the success of your vision.** Your vision can change but your ethics and your core values should not change. How you treat people, how you address people, how you talk to people, how you deal with people, whether or not you're honest with people, are all reflections from the mirror of your value system. Standing for something matters. Your stance should be proactive and emulate who you are. I've seen people do anything to get ahead and even more to earn a dollar. They don't care if they hurt people along the way. This is dangerous. Your personal integrity is more important than your personal net worth.

# GET RICH QUICK?

Maybe your vision is to do a particular project that you know is good and you have devoted countless hours and energy into the project; you really believe

in it, but the only clincher is the fact that it may take time for it to secure funding. During these times it's very easy to become distracted. I was approached years ago to form a business partnership

with some professional people I knew. I listened as they shared their vision to launch this money-making business. They were excited about the lucrative opportunity but something about their strategy did not sit well with me. I simply didn't trust their judgment nor their business tactics so I decided that joining forces with them would not be in the best interest of Juliette, Inc. I graciously declined their offer. Needless to say, their business practices ended up warranting a legal investigation and things did not end well. I'm glad that I didn't assume that because I knew these people, I should go into business with them. Sometimes good people make bad decisions.

You can't afford to get sidetracked by quick schemes and get-rich scams that ultimately exploit other people. Your brand carries too much weight to attach itself to just anything. Your name and your brand has to stand it's ground and say "I will not be a part of this." I will wait it out and stick to my vision. My father had every opportunity to take advantage of the community that did not have easy access to fresh fruits and vegetables, but instead he chose to establish an honest brand, thus building a business that funded the college experience for me and my sister. Without a degree or corporate experience, my father's life and wisdom taught me the greatest lessons.

# CONSIDER THIS!

What lessons do you need to point to when it's time to stand your ground and do the right thing versus the more convenient or lucrative thing?

_____

_____

_____

_____

_____

_____

_____

_____

_____

_____

_____

How have assumptions gotten you off course in the past?

_____

_____

_____

_____

_____

_____

_____

_____

_____

_____

_____

_____

_____

_____

_____

*Chapter 7*

# Adapt To and Manage Change

# adapt to and manage change

W e've all been told that change is good and we should accept it, create it and embrace it. The list of phrases is endless and change management initiatives in the workplace are key strategies for many successful businesses. But how does adapting and managing change apply to You, Inc.

How we perceive change will fundamentally effect how we respond to it. If we view change as a bad thing, then naturally we will resist the possibility of anything good occurring as a result of it. Change gives us an opportunity to grow. The challenge

---

*If we view change as a bad thing, then naturally we will resist the possibility of anything good occurring as a result of it. Change gives us an opportunity to grow.*

---

provides strength training for otherwise weakened character muscles. It's really all about how you view the moving and shifting parts around you. How can you guide change in a way that transfers the control back to you? To start, you can't wait until things collapse to get moving, you must look for the signs and prepare so that you can find a space at the front of the line.

# THE WRITING ON THE WALL

I contend that there are always signs that change is on the horizon, so read the writing on the wall. Don't wait for things to fall apart and then play the role of the victim who is swept away by a big tide. A sign could be small, like a few changes in the board of directors of your company, or big, like a 10% pay cut.

My signal was big--- a 10% pay cut in my city government paycheck. I enjoyed my work and I was making significant contributions to civic life by leading a number of high profile projects. My reputation was growing in a good way. The day I got the salary news was the day that I started planning a pathway to my goal: a position in the private sector. There were no growth opportunities in city government. It was time to move on. I knew that this would not be a swift process. I had to exercise patience to execute my plan. Ultimately, it took two years for me to make that first step to a new private sector position.

Along with the negative salary adjustment, I realized that the mayor I was currently serving would not seek re-election. He had made it possible for me to build a body of work that was respected. In short, he was a huge "unofficial" mentor. The new leaders would bring in their own team, and that would most likely not include me! That was enough information for me. I watched other colleagues, convinced that their government salaries would be restored, muddle along as if everything was fine. Some had developed an overblown since of importance and thought that no one had the power to demote them or their positions.

Unfortunately, everyone who adopted one of these aforementioned approaches experienced fatal career setbacks. Meanwhile my strategy was threefold. I decided that I would:

### 1. REPORT TO MY POSITION AND CONTINUE TO WORK HARD:

I worked as diligently as ever, even though the work place had changed dramatically. I was not the "go-to" girl, but I was someone from the old regime who no one wanted to talk to. I cleaned my office files and prepared for my departure.

### 2. DEVELOP AN EXCELLENT RESUME:

My goal was to transition from the public sector to the private sector. I had a PhD, but I had spent 15 years in city government, making for a pretty dull work history at first glance. I had reported some major projects, and also had international work experience. Getting a professional writer to craft the right resume was well worth the investment, and I use

---

*Change is a process that each of us will have to endure, even if we are afraid.*

---

that template to this day. The writer that I contracted had a special talent for interviewing and writing the resume in a way that made the accomplishments sing on the paper. Don't construct your resume on your own--- this is your first impression, don't make it your last!

### 3. Tell anyone who would listen that I was seeking a new job:

How can you get help if your life is a big secret? I had a patented fifteen second elevator speech about the current and future goals of Juliette, Inc. I used any opportunity to share that I was searching for a position in the corporate world. If someone said "Hello, how are you today?", my response was "I'm great, but really excited about expanding my horizons to the corporate realm---I know it will be tough but I need all the referrals I can get... and how are you?"

# No magic wand

In life there is no magic wand. You can't wave the change away. You can't close your eyes really tight and wish that change won't happen, and your wish be granted. Just as there are four seasons that must occur during each year as a result of the earth being tilted on its axis with respect to its orbital plane… such is life, work and the relationships around you.

Change is a process that each of us will have to endure, even if we are afraid. Beware of the fear that lurks around when change comes on the scene. Fear of the unknown will detonate any possibility for forward movement. Change is going to happen. Expect it and prepare for it as best you can. People that learn to manage change well, find excitement in the not knowing. They look for the white canvas to create because change forces them to think and behave differently.

## Moving to Higher Ground

I love to share the fact that my daughter changed me for the better, bringing more clarity, a sense of purpose, and ambition to my life.  It was clear, early on, that school would be difficult for her because she had a learning challenge.  This challenge is a task for the parent and the  child to manage.  We both embraced it!!  Juliette, Inc. had no time for a pity party.  There were rough days, but with help from family, friends, and educators, we made it through. In fact, my daughter has won awards for her leadership skills, including being named as one of 2,000 Millennium Dreamers, a global initiative co-sponsored by the Disney and McDonald's Corporations in 2000, the dawn of the new century.  As a family, we let go of the limitations, embrace who we are, and we live our lives with transparency. We moved Juliette, Inc. to higher ground because of it.

I can lay out the groundwork and instruct you to follow all the 10 things as they are scripted in this book, but you will find out that life doesn't work that smoothly. Even if you think you have

*When you decide to use your mind to create something bigger and better, you can come through the changes of life stronger than ever. It takes courage to manage the change that is transpiring all around you.*

a winning hand, many times because of all kinds of circumstances, personal setbacks or something just pops out from nowhere--change finds its way into your life without an invitation. Sometimes the circumstances surrounding change can completely knock you off your feet to the point where you start to forget exactly what you were doing. You stop thinking about yourself as being You, Inc. You stop feeling like you're responsible for yourself because too many people are pushing and pulling you in different directions and you don't seem to have a grasp on that little part that you can control which is your own mind. You've crafted your vision and now you're being forced to tweak the vision or put it on the shelf for a moment.

You might be asking yourself, When can I be in control again? When you decide to use your mind to create something bigger and better, you can come through the changes of life stronger than ever. It takes courage to manage the change that is transpiring all around you. The magic wand doesn't work, but your brilliant mind does. Make the changes in your life work for you. Don't be afraid!

# CONSIDER THIS!

Do you feel vulnerable when unexpected changes occur?

_____

_____

_____

_____

_____

_____

What is your typical response to change? How can you improve this?

_____

_____

_____

_____

_____

# Chapter 8

# Always Have Something to Say

# always have something to say

A conversation should never be forgotten or wasted time. Your conversation with others can be productive and should be full of giveaways and takeaways. Whether you are talking to a stranger or a colleague, you should have something of value to contribute to the dialogue.

No one likes a "know it all" and quite frankly some of us are annoyed by people who don't have an original thought. However, I believe that the aptitude for mastery in this area lies in your ability to find a way to initiate meaning in the connections. You must be willing to engage with them by leaving them with a piece of you and giving them an opportunity to uncover a piece of themselves. It all starts with reading your audience carefully so as not to offend the listeners.

It's important to respect communication styles and be aware of gender differences as you strive to enhance your communication style. The objective is to have meaningful dialogue, not empty, lifeless conversation.

You have to quickly affirm people, this draws them in and before you know it, they are listening to you.

To affirm a person and find common ground is easier than we think. We simply have to pay attention. Look and listen for details from their world and acknowledge them. If you're in your boss's office and you notice pictures of fishing

> *Throughout the conversation you should be making mental notes and filing them away for later.*

tackle, that's a detail that can become the source of engagement. You have to give them the space to talk about themselves. It's a tactic that you can use to start the conversation but it must be genuine. When a person is no longer looking at the clock during the conversation with you, you have walked into a wide space, and this becomes your room to make the connection and insert your ideas or thoughts into the dialogue. Throughout the conversation you should be making mental notes

*What if you've missed opportunities because your conversation never gave them space to emerge?*

and filing them away for later. When you see this person again you should reference the connection point in conversation. For example, you would revisit the person's passion for fishing once you saw them again. Remember it's about giveaways and takeaways.

## A NEW JOB REFERRAL

During a conversation with a colleague, I mentioned that I was about to start looking for a new position.

We talked about her experience and what she wanted to do in her career first. Then, I said, "You know, I've been thinking it might be a good idea for me to start looking around, if you hear about something please let me know." Well, a few months later someone was recruiting her for a position and in an off-hand comment they mentioned that they were also looking for someone to work in the field that I worked in.

She recommended me to them. I must interject here that initially my colleague did not want to work with me on a particular project. She was not my biggest fan, but during this conversation we managed to meet in a common place regarding the fact that our work environment was very challenging. She became my spokesperson at the right moment. She came back to me and said "I encouraged the recruiter to talk to you. I told them that you were really good." I got the job, but it started with the fact that I had something to say. What if you've missed opportunities because your conversation never offered a chance for others' opinions to emerge?

Here's my conversation model. I always present people with a challenge, an opportunity, and a status about myself all while listening and giving them space to share. When presenting a challenge in the conversation, you give the person an opportunity to form a connection with you by offering an unknown or something they hadn't considered. In a personal conversation it could be the fact that you share something from your life experience. For example, sharing that you have an upcoming doctor's visit and the nervousness that you feel as the appointment approaches. In a corporate setting, I always employ this strategy during an interview.

For starters, I'm always prepared. I create a binder specific to the job that I'm applying for. I study the company and the job description. I try to identify the challenge before the interview. In this instance, I would acknowledge the fact that I had reviewed the company's collateral material and the website and I love the way the content flows, but I noticed the color palettes are different for the website and the brochures. In both scenarios, you've presented a challenge and created an opportunity for yourself within the dialogue.

Sharing the detail about your life in the personal conversation invites more dialogue and forms a connection between you and the listener, thus creating an opportunity. In the interview, you have created a space where you can insert how you can provide a solution for the company. Are you getting this? Conversations are not just for talking, they should be meaningful and productive. Throughout this process, you should be actively listening and giving the other party an opportunity to share.

Now that you have their attention, you can toss in a status about yourself. i.e. "I've started juicing, and it's helping me to reclaim my health. I'm rewarding myself with good health." Or "About three years ago, I helped to develop marketing collateral for an employer that helped to establish our brand online in a more effective way." Remember great conversations should include giveaways and takeaways. I sincerely believe that it's what you give to people in a moment that makes your interaction with them most memorable.

# CONVERSATION MODEL

**1) Offer A Challenge**- Opportunity to form a connection by offering an unknown or something someone hadn't considered.

**2) Create Opportunity**-Sharing details about your life in a personal conversation invites more dialogue and forms a connection between you and the listener, thus creating an opportunity.

**3) Status Update**- Now that you have their attention, you can toss in a status about yourself.

# CONSIDER THIS!

Does anyone remember talking to you?

_____

_____

_____

_____

_____

_____

Describe what strangers might say about their initial conversation with you?

_____

_____

_____

_____

_____

# *Chapter 9*

# Look for the Win-Win

# look for the win-win

A few years ago, a new reality show emerged called The Biggest Loser. The show features the weight-loss journey of its contestants. Each contestant has a substantial amount of weight to lose. The person losing the highest percentage of weight becomes "The Biggest Loser" and ultimately the winner. The winner receives a cash prize for all of their hard work throughout the season, they appear on the cover of magazines and sit on the couches of talk show hosts as one who is esteemed and respected for their accomplishment.

In life, there really is no win for you if someone else is the "biggest loser." I've found my greatest victories come when others cross the finish line with me. Looking for that "middle-ground" so all involved get the best outcome, is not only mature but it's wise. A winning attitude is so much more than simply saying "I can", it's about helping someone realize that they can too.

Winners aren't afraid of opposition because they can see a success trail just beyond the tension.

*I've found my greatest victories come when others cross the finish line with me.*

## Beyond the tension

The inherent tension that comes as a result of everyday living can either stretch us to a place that causes us to experience greatness or it can cause us to snap from the pressure. Winners find a sweet spot just beyond the tension. I've managed to remain in opportunity-seeking mode as Juliette, Inc., even when it does not appear so to others, especially my employer!

## Mountaintop and valley times

In the course of my professional career, I have had mountain-top experiences where it seemed as

though I was a magnet for everything good.

But, I've also had valley experiences where things were not as I'd hoped for. During the low times, I had to fight the tendency to focus inward. When you do that, you release more venom to the bite.

The ability to identify a win-win calls for a positive and selfless approach. Start by searching for a way that gives everyone the chance to win something.

*The ability to identify a win-win takes a positive and selfless approach.*

While struggling professionally in my career, I decided to stop complaining about my situation and frustrations and instead reach out to help others within the company. In one of my professional roles, I started a mentoring program.

The mentoring program supported twenty mid-level managers. All of them had a personal goal, and that was "getting promoted." The program included people who were young, rising stars and seasoned

professionals who had for some reason become "stuck" in their careers. The group was a great mix by age, ethnicity and gender.

I wanted to help them, but I knew that the first step toward promotion had to begin with shifting the focus from "me" to "us" or the group. After the orientation session, we started monthly group meetings. Each participant received a binder that included readings, assignments and a calendar of scheduled activities.

Each participant was assigned a mentor from the executive team, and they also met monthly, or more often, if desired.

*The job in Nigeria wasn't just a professional win but it was a personal win for me as well.*

Volunteer events were scheduled and mandatory "fun" community/civic activities were included. These events were vital to establishing a community of professionals that could exist and function as a team. This experience taught me the power of turning my thoughts to service and leadership, instead of the next move up the ladder. This got me promoted faster! It worked for me and I knew it would work for them, and it did. I couldn't navigate my own rough seas, but I launched a row boat to bring others safely to shore.

# ADJUST YOUR SAILS

Jimmy Dean said "I can't change the direction of the wind, but I can adjust my sails to always reach my destination." Sometimes it takes a simple adjustment in our thinking and our plan to yield a better score. In more ways than one, I've been stopped or stymied in my career growth. Each time I had to recalibrate my brain, and think like a winner. Winners happen to see the win bigger than the possibility of failure.

At one time in my career, the adjustment of my sails included working overseas. This was such a huge decision for me, many questioned if it was the best move for me to make. Early on, I realized that everyone may not see the value in your decisions, but if you believe that something is best for you, keep moving in that direction. I expected that some things would be challenging because of my decision to live and work in Nigeria, but nothing prepared me for what I would experience and how my life would change forever.

# THE MOVE TO AFRICA

I was 28-years-old preparing to embark on my first trip to Africa. I would be living in a new country, new city and new neighborhood where I knew no one. Nothing was familiar and I had no idea how to navigate. When I arrived in Nigeria, after hours of travel, I became sick. After a few days I made the right connections to see a health practitioner who nursed me back to good health in a short time.

I was then ready to work. As the only American and female on the project team, I gained respect from my colleagues. I worked hard and listened intently. I learned invaluable lessons about navigating cultural norms, customs and values. I made great friends in a place where I knew no one. So many of the circumstances surrounding this move had created nagging thoughts  that perhaps this was not a good decision, but it was a great decision. This opportunity gave my career and self-esteem a life changing boost. Moving to Nigeria helped me to believe in myself. Nigeria has been a gift that continues to resonate in my life, from the friends and colleagues I've gained to providing me with the confidence and experiences that motivate me to take big chances.

The job in Nigeria wasn't just a professional win but it was a personal win for me as well. My eyes and ears were forever changed about how I process information and make judgments about others. I learned how to conduct business in a foreign land. I placed value on the relationships that were formed, and I allowed the experience to teach me something new. I soaked in the knowledge I was learning about business but also learned about my African heritage and the things that helped shape my character as a person. My Nigerian employer "won" in having me on the team of professionals who made a tremendous impact in the work we were producing. And, I "won" too. The job opportunity helped to facilitate my growth, and the people of Nigeria helped shape me into the woman I am today. My sails led me to Africa and the wind is still carrying me.

# CONSIDER THIS!

Where is the wind carrying you? _____

_____

_____

_____

_____

_____

_____

Is it time to adjust your sail? _____

_____

_____

_____

_____

_____

_____

# Chapter 10

# Success is the Best Revenge

# success is the best revenge

F rank Sinatra is quoted as saying-- "the best revenge is massive success." This philosophy takes the focus off others and shifts it directly to you. Plotting and scheming to get back at another person should never be the goal. It's about living your vision in a way that produces an exception to the limitations seemingly imposed by others or systems that have worked against you. You see, it's your life and you're in control of how you respond when faced with unfavorable circumstances. My suggestion to you is to live your vision and allow the success to flow from that place.

## THE "AFFAIR" THAT NEVER HAPPENED

During my professional career, I have experienced various degrees of unfairness, backstabbing, sexual harassment and racism. When the world around me was cruel and unjust, in an effort to guard my heart and protect my brand, I chose success for Juliette, Inc. as the ultimate revenge.

---

*You see, it's your life and you're in control of how you respond when faced with unfavorable circumstances.*

---

I vowed to never get back at a person, or prevent someone from moving forward. In fact, instead of tripping up the married senior board member who propositioned me inappropriately, I decided to maintain a cordial, professional relationship … and it worked!

Yes, it was offensive and annoying when he made remarks loaded with sexual innuendo, but that all ceased quickly as I remained strategic and focused. I simply decided to live out my vision every day and defy the unfair rules of the marketplace culture. I was determined to be successful and kind. Assertive and generous. A leader and a great team player. I simply became brutally honest with this powerful man about my convictions and refused him.

Then I diverted his attention by helping him push his agenda forward. Amazingly, today we are friends. He's mentored and helped me without any sexual element in our relationship. It really wasn't about sex in the first place, it was about power. My approach isn't always easy. I really hope I'm not painting that picture, but it is a decision each individual must make for themselves. And it's one you may have to revisit a few times throughout

*Choose to help those who come at you in a disrespectful way by changing the lens and making sure that you don't fall into the ditch that they are in!*

your life. Choose to help those who come at you in a disrespectful way by changing the lens and making sure that you don't fall into the ditch that they are in!

I chose my own success over planning anyone's demise. I go to bed every night with a clear conscience, at peace with myself and others. Traveling the road of peace has great rewards.

Throughout this process, you will have to make the decision for peace very quickly before negative thoughts have time to get settled in your mind and in your heart. During my tenure at one company, my boss had been involved in several situations that were dishonest, some of which had directly affected me, and were coming back to haunt him.

One day while driving in my car I received a phone call from him. During the conversation, he disclosed in great detail the dilemma he was facing and asked me what he should do to fix the situation. In that moment, I was confronted with a major decision. Either I could focus on all of the negative things that had transpired under his leadership or I could report to my position.

That day I decided to "show up" and help him. I pulled

over on the side of the road and talked him through a strategy that involved him being honest and integral. He followed my advice and was able to successfully reestablish a key connection with a community leader. I chose the right path and this road continued to lead me to more success.

Success for me is the reflection of the good all around me. I can protect my brand by doing a good job and by being good to others. In turn, the stock value of Juliette, Inc. increases with each act of kindness, and my perpetual decision to challenge myself and push others in a positive direction. Life isn't always fair and people sometimes change the rules of the game when you're winning, but these ten things have kept me grounded and on a steady track to reach my goals and live my vision. I love the way my success looks and feels, and you will too! Tweak my advice, make it your own.

# CONSIDER THIS!

What good are you reflecting?_____

_____

_____

_____

_____

_____

How are you improving other people?_____

_____

_____

_____

_____

_____

When was the last time you displayed forgiveness?

_____

_____

_____

_____

Kindness?_____

How have you challenged yourself and others to keep pushing forward?

_____

_____

_____

_____

_____

_____

# ABOUT THE AUTHOR

In "10 Things I Know" Juliette Okotie-Eboh, PhD shares the 10 things she's come to know as truth in her first published book after a professional career spanning over 30 years working in healthcare, city government, banking, international business and most recently over a decade as Senior Vice President for one of the largest gaming corporations in the United States.

She's taught on the university level, served on numerous civic boards and managed urban planning and international economic research projects. She's directed work teams, reported to company presidents and transitioned from city government work to non-profit and private sector assignments. These varied professional experiences afforded her the opportunity to maneuver and achieve high levels of professional success.

Her passion today is to share the "secrets" that shaped her journey to the "C-Suite" with others. She actively gives herself to mentoring women's groups as well as training and developing mid-managers and line workers who are striving for more.

# DERE PUBLISHING

Visit thedrjuliette.com to learn more about Dr. Juliette's workshops and training courses surrounding the 10 THINGS concepts.

# Ten Things I Know

*Corporate conversations for personal growth and professional development with Dr. Juliette*

### The Ten Things Workshop

"The Ten Things I Know" workshop will guide participants through an inspiring and refreshing journey on the principles of the Ten Things I Know book. Dr. Juliette makes the presentation flexible for audiences ranging from entry level employees to C-suite executives.

### The Ten Things Experience

"The Ten Things I Know" experience is an intensely

focused small group training session specifically designed for more interaction among participants and Dr. Juliette. This small group forum allows more "air time" for participants to express opinions, contribute ideas, ask questions and learn from each other

### The Ten Things Intensive (Women Only)

Women who work in corporate and government sectors quickly identify with Ten Things I Know. This workshop is more than a "how to climb the corporate ladder" guide, but a frank conversation with the audience to reflect on how to make Ten Things I Know work for them.

**DERE**publishing

## FOR SPEAKING ENGAGEMENTS

Diane Palmer

DP Marketing Strategies

tel: 832.304.4326

email: dpalmer@dpmarketingstrategies.com